Grade Tv

Ukulele
Playing

Compiled by

RGT.

Registry of Guitar Tutors

www.RGT.org

Printed and bound in Great Britain

A CIP record for this publication is available from the British Library
ISBN: 978-1-905908-52-3

Published by Registry Publications

Registry Mews, Wilton Rd, Bexhill, Sussex, TN40 1HY

Text, all musical compositions and arrangements by Tony Skinner.
Music typesetting, additional text and editing by Merv Young.
Design and photography by JAK Images.

Compiled for

Registry of Guitar Tutors

www.RGT.org

v.20140807

Contents

CD track listing

Introduction

This handbook is part of a progressive series of handbooks primarily intended for candidates considering taking a Registry Of Guitar Tutors (RGT) exam in ukulele playing. However, the series also provides a solid foundation of musical education for any ukulele student – whether intending to take an exam or not.

The RGT exams recognise the fact that some ukulele players focus on the ukulele wholly in terms of its role as a chordal/rhythm playing instrument, while other ukulele players prefer to also explore the melody playing potential of the instrument. Consequently, the syllabus structure has been designed so that it can be utilised with equal success by candidates who are developing both melody and rhythm playing skills, as well as by those candidates who are focusing solely on chordal/rhythm playing techniques.

TUNING

This exam is designed for Soprano (a.k.a 'standard'), Concert and Tenor ukulele players that use standard G C E A tuning.

The use of an electronic tuner or other tuning aid, prior to, or at the start of the exam, is permitted.

FRETBOXES

Fretboxes are used to illustrate the chords required at this level.

Vertical lines represent the strings – with the line furthest to the right representing the high A string. Horizontal lines represent the frets.

The numbers on the lines show the recommended fingering: 1 represents the index finger; 2 = the long middle finger; 3 = the ring finger; 4 = the little finger.

0 above a string line indicates that an open (unfretted) string should be played.

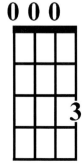

This example means you should press with the third finger at the third fret on the A string; the other strings should be played open.

FINGERING OPTIONS

Throughout the exam, it is entirely the candidate's choice as to whether a pick (plectrum) or fingers or a combination of both are used to strum/pick the strings, the only exception being if the Fingerstyle Study is played during Section Three.

The fret-hand fingerings that are shown in this handbook are those that are most likely to be effective for the widest range of players at this level. However, there are a variety of alternative fingerings that could be used, and any that produce an effective musical result will be acceptable; there is no requirement to use the exact fingerings shown within this handbook.

MELODY NOTATION

Melodies are notated using both traditional musical notation and tablature. The basics of tablature are explained below:

Tablature:

Horizontal lines represent the strings (with the top line being the high A string). The numbers on the string lines refer to the frets. 0 on a line means play that string open (unfretted).

The example below means play at the third fret on the A string.

CHORD SYMBOLS

This handbook (and exam) use the following standard abbreviations when referring to chords:

• The symbol for a major chord is the capital letter of the name of the chord. For example, the symbol for G major is **G**.

• The symbol for a minor chord is the capital letter of the name of the chord plus lower case m. For example, the symbol for G minor is **Gm**.

• The symbol for a dominant seventh chord is the capital letter of the name of the chord followed by 7. For example, the symbol for G dominant seventh is **G7**.

• The symbol for a minor seventh chord is the capital letter of the name of the chord followed by m7. For example, the symbol for G minor seventh is **Gm7**.

• The symbol for a major seventh chord is the capital letter of the name of the chord followed by maj7. For example, the symbol for C major seventh is **Cmaj7**.

EXAM TYPES & FORMAT

RGT offers two types of exam for individual ukulele candidates: **Grade Exams** (this handbook covers the material required for the Grade Two Exam) and **Performance Awards** (this handbook covers the material required for the Level Two Performance Award).

The Grade Two Exam contains the following sections:

- Section 1:   Rhythm Study

- Section 2:   Performance

- Section 3:   Free Choice Specialism

- Section 4:   Prepared Accompaniment

- Section 5:   Musicianship

A maximum of 20 marks may be awarded for each section.

The Level Two Performance Award does not include the Musicianship section, but instead focuses on performance by requiring two pieces (rather than one as in the grade exam) to be played during the Free Choice Specialism section. The remainder of the requirements for the Level Two Performance Award are exactly the same as those for the Grade Two Exam. In the Performance Award a maximum of 20 marks may be awarded for each piece performed.

Grade exams are traditional 'live' exams, where the candidate attends an exam venue at an allotted time and date. However, with Performance Awards three options are available. These are described overleaf.

1. **_Live Performance Award:_** the candidate attends an exam venue and performs their pieces.

2. **_Filmed Performance Award:_** this follows the same format as a Live Performance Award, except that the candidate submits a video recording of their performances rather than attending an exam venue. The video may be submitted on DVD or uploaded via the RGT website. A slightly higher standard of performance will be expected than for a Live Performance Award.

3. **_Recorded Performance Award:_** this follows the same format as a Live Performance Award, except that the candidate submits an audio recording of their performances rather than attending an exam venue. The recording may be submitted on CD or uploaded via the RGT website. A significantly higher standard of performance will be expected than for a Live Performance Award.

Performance Awards are designed for those who prefer to focus on performing pieces. The Filmed and Recorded Performance Awards are also particularly useful for those who find it hard to take time off for an exam or to travel to an exam venue, or for those who get overly nervous in an exam situation, as performances can be submitted by disc or uploaded online without the need to attend an exam venue.

In addition to exams for individuals, RGT also offers ensemble exams for ukulele. For more details see the RGT website www.RGT.org

EXAM ENTRY

Grade Two Exam:
An exam entry form is provided at the rear of this handbook. This is the only valid entry form for the RGT ukulele Grade Two exam.

Please note that if the entry form is detached and lost, it will not be replaced under any circumstances and the candidate will be required to obtain a replacement handbook to obtain another entry form.

The entry form includes a unique entry code to enable you to enter online via the RGT website www.RGT.org

Level Two Performance Award:
The entry form and further information about Performance Awards can be downloaded from the RGT website www.RGT.org

Rhythm Study

You should select and play <u>ONE</u> of the four Rhythm Studies from this chapter, using the notated strum pattern.

Performances do not need to be from memory: the handbook may be used during this section of the exam. Remember to bring your handbook to the exam if you do not intend to play from memory; photocopies will not be permitted.

• Each Rhythm Study consists of a 12-bar chord progression in either $^4_4$ or $^3_4$ time that should be played twice before ending on the key chord. (The two sets of vertical dots at the start of bar 1 and at the end of bar 12 indicate the section to be repeated.)

• The notated strum pattern should be reproduced exactly throughout the entire first verse. However, during the repeat section some musically suitable rhythmic variation of your own choosing should be used. At this grade, the variation(s) used needn't be too complex and could be a different strum pattern repeated throughout the repeat section or alternatively some rhythmic variation could be used only in certain bars of the repeat section to act as a musical contrast. The more musically effective the variation used is the higher the mark that may be awarded.

• Note that on the CD recordings only the first verse (and final chord) have been recorded; the verse where a variation should be used has not been included on the recording. This has been done deliberately in order to encourage candidates to experiment and develop their own ideas for variations and prevent them just copying a recorded example.

• The final closing bar (after the repeat section) should be played with just a single strum.

• Either a pick (plectrum) or fingers, or a combination of both, can be used to strum the strings – it is your choice. You should also decide which combination of downstrokes and upstrokes will achieve the most effective musical result.

• Tempo indications are for general guidance – performances at slightly slower or faster tempos will be acceptable.

CHORDS

The range of chords that may occur at this level, include those listed for previous grades – i.e.:

A C D F G   Am Dm Gm   A7 C7 E7 G7

Plus, those newly introduced at this grade:

Bb Em F#m D7 Cmaj7 Gm7

Fretboxes showing the fingering for these chords are provided below:

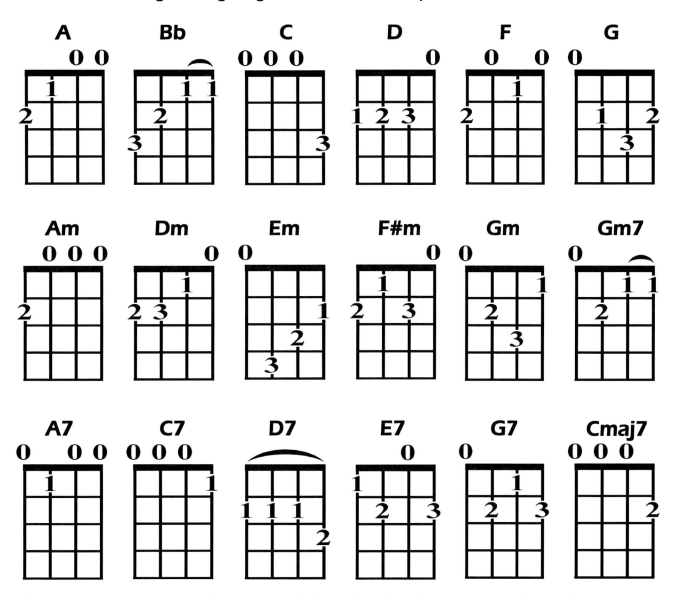

You are not required to use the same chord shape fingerings that are shown above. For example, depending upon the surrounding chords, it may sometimes be easier to change chord if Am is fretted using the 1st finger instead of the 2nd.

In the fretboxes above, Bb, Gm7 and D7 employ the 1st finger laying flat to fret more than one string simultaneously; if preferred, these chords could be re-fingered to avoid this technique.

Alternative fingerings will be acceptable for any chords provided that the chords themselves are technically accurate and that the chord voicings combine with each other in a musical effective way.

RHYTHM STUDY ADVICE

In order to achieve the most musical performance and obtain a high mark in this section of the exam, you should aim for the following when performing the Rhythm Study:

• A secure knowledge of the chord shapes, so that you can play the chords accurately.

• The ability to change from one chord shape to another smoothly and without hesitation or delay.

• Clear sounding chords that are free of fretbuzz and any unintended muting of notes.

• A fluent rhythm style, maintaining an even tempo throughout.

• Accurate reproduction of the rhythm of the notated strum pattern during the first verse. Where accent marks are included in the notation for the strum pattern (i.e. in Rhythm Studies 2 and 4), ensure that the chords on the accented beats are played more strongly. Also, ensure that the remaining strums are played at a more natural volume level, so that the effect of the accented chords can be clearly heard.

• Use of some variation(s) to the notated strum pattern during the repeat section to enhance the overall musical effect of the performance. The variation could involve, for example, playing either a busier or, conversely, a slightly less busy pattern throughout the repeat section or just in certain bars of the repeat section. Any variation used should retain some musical connection to the original strum pattern and should not be over-simplified just to make the performance easier.

RHYTHM STUDY NO. 1

♩ = 116

| $\frac{4}{4}$‖: **E**m | | **A**m | **E**m | **D** | **C** | **C**maj7 | |

| **A**m | **D**7 | **G** | **C** | **A**m | **D** | :‖**E**m | ‖ |

Strum pattern:

This rhythm study is in $^4_4$ time. The notated strum pattern indicates that you should play on the following underlined beats: <u>1</u> (&) (2) <u>& 3 & 4</u> (&)

LISTEN AND LEARN: Rhythm Study No. 1 can be heard on CD track 1

RHYTHM STUDY NO. 2

♩ = 108

| $\frac{4}{4}$‖: **F** | **B**♭ | **F** | **C** | **G**m | **G**m7 | |

| **A** | **A**7 | **D**m | **B**♭ | **C** | **C**7 | :‖**F** | |

Strum pattern:

This rhythm study is in $^4_4$ time. The notated strum pattern indicates that you should play on the following underlined beats: <u>1</u> & <u>2</u> & <u>3</u> & <u>4</u> (&)

The small arrowheads underneath beats 2 and 4 are 'accent' marks to indicate that the chords on these beats should be played more strongly.

LISTEN AND LEARN: Rhythm Study No. 2 can be heard on CD track 2

RHYTHM STUDY NO. 3

♩ = 92

| $\frac{3}{4}$ ‖: D | | A | | F♯m | | G | | D | | Em | |

| A | | A7 | | G | | F♯m | | Em | | A | :‖ D | |

Strum pattern:

This Rhythm Study is in $^3_4$ time – meaning that there are three main beats per bar. The notated strum pattern indicates that you should play on the following underlined beats: **1** (&) (2) **& 3** (&)

LISTEN AND LEARN: Rhythm Study No. 3 can be heard on CD track 3

RHYTHM STUDY NO. 4

♩ = 116

| $\frac{4}{4}$ ‖: G | | D | | C | | D | | G | | Em | |

| Am | | D | | Cmaj7 | | C | | D | | D7 | :‖ G | |

Strum pattern:

The notated strum pattern for this rhythm study, in $^4_4$ time, indicates that you should play on all four beats, but with an extra strum added after beats 2 and 4 – i.e. you should play on the following underlined beats: **1** (&) **2 & 3** (&) **4 &**

The small arrowheads underneath beats 2 and 4 are 'accent' marks to indicate that the chords on these beats should be played more strongly.

LISTEN AND LEARN: Rhythm Study No. 4 can be heard on CD track 4

Performance

There are two options to choose from in this section of the exam, and you are free to select which of these options you prefer.

OPTION 1

Play a melody:

You should select and perform <u>ONE</u> of the four melodies provided in this chapter.

OR

OPTION 2

Play another Rhythm Study:

If you prefer to focus on rhythm playing rather than melody playing, you can select another Rhythm Study from the previous chapter. This chord chart should then be performed either using the notated strum pattern provided with it or, if you prefer, you can use a musically appropriate rhythm of your own choosing, providing that it is of at least a similar technical standard to the notated rhythms. As indicated in the Rhythm Studies chapter earlier in this handbook, during the repeat section of the rhythm study some musically suitable rhythmic variation of your own choosing should be used.

If selecting this option, the chord chart that is performed must be a different one from that played in the earlier section of the exam.

If you decide to choose 'Option 2' refer to the previous Rhythm Study chapter for all the information you will require; the remainder of this chapter refers to 'Option 1' – i.e. playing a melody.

MELODY

You can select and play ONE of the four melodies notated on the following pages. You do not need to play from memory: the handbook may be used during this section of the exam. Remember to bring your handbook to the exam if you do not intend to play from memory; photocopies will not be permitted.

- The melody can be played with a pick or using fingers – it's your choice.

- Tempo markings have been chosen that reflect the capabilities expected at this level, but are for general guidance only: faster, or slightly slower, tempos can be used providing they produce an effective musical result.

- The melody must be played unaccompanied. Chord symbols are provided for each melody purely to enable a teacher or fellow player to provide accompaniment during practice. You are NOT required to play the chords in this section of the exam – only the melody, unaccompanied. (On the CD an accompaniment is provided to each melody only to enhance the musical effect and reinforce the timing for learning purposes.)

MELODY PLAYING ADVICE

In order to achieve the most musical performance and obtain a high mark in the exam you should aim for the following when performing your chosen melody:

- An accurate reproduction of the pitch of the melody.

- An accurate reproduction of the timing of the rhythm of the melody.

- A fluent rendition, without pauses or hesitation.

- Maintaining an even tempo throughout.

- Clear sounding notes that are free of fretbuzz.

- Capturing the phrasing within the melody.

- Accurate observation of the repeat markings.

- A confident performance that demonstrates some stylistic awareness.

- Some use of dynamics where musically appropriate.

Autumn Lament

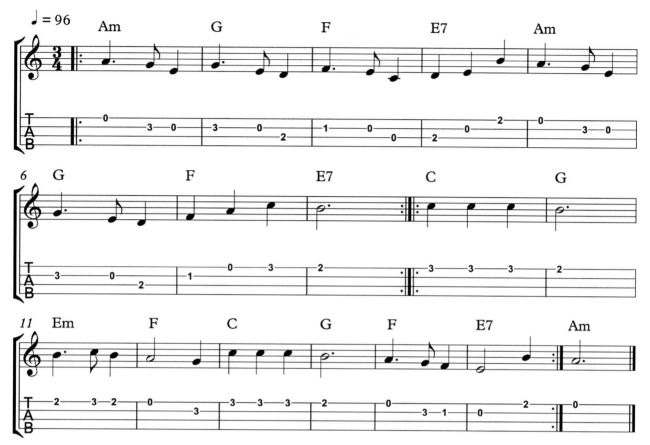

Playing Guide:

- This melody is in $\frac{3}{4}$ time. It is in two 8-bar sections, both of which should be repeated – as indicated by the sets of vertical dots that appear. The first section is from bar 1 to 8 and the second section is from bar 9 to 16. The piece then ends in bar 17.

- The melody is notated in the key of A minor and all the notes are from the A natural minor scale.

- A distinctive characteristic of this melody is the use of the dotted rhythm that appears in a number of bars, such as in the first three bars. The dotted rhythm means that instead of playing evenly on beats 1, 2 and 3, the length of the first (dotted) note is extended, whilst the second note is shortened – creating a rhythm of <u>1</u> (2)<u>&</u> <u>3</u>.

LISTEN AND LEARN: Autumn Lament can be heard on CD track 5

Home On The Range

This arrangement © copyright 2014 by Registry Publications

Playing Guide:

- This melody is in ³₄ time. It begins on beat 3 (i.e. after a count of 2). Notice that there are a number of 'tied' notes, where the note should be allowed to ring into the next bar as indicated (e.g. from bar 7 into bar 8).

- The melody features two different sections, the second of which should be repeated – as indicated by the sets of vertical dots that appear in bars 17 and 32.

- The melody is notated in the key of F major and the notes all come from the F major scale. This key includes the note Bb, which is played on fret 1 of the first (A) string.

LISTEN AND LEARN: Home On The Range can be heard on CD track 6

Drunken Sailor

This arrangement © copyright 2014 by Registry Publications

Playing Guide:

- This melody is arranged in $\frac{4}{4}$ time. It is in two 8-bar sections, both of which should be repeated – as indicated by the sets of vertical dots that appear. The first section is from bar 1 to 8 and the second section is from bar 9 to 16.

- The melody is notated using an E minor key signature. However, the melody does contain a C# note (in bars 6 and 14) which means that the melody is derived from the E Dorian modal scale; a minor modal scale which is commonly used in traditional folk tunes.

LISTEN AND LEARN: Drunken Sailor can be heard on CD track 7

Galway Gallop

Playing Guide:

- This melody is in $^4_4$ time. It begins on beat 4 (i.e. after a count of 3). The first four full bars are repeated.

- The melody is notated in the key of G major and all the notes are from the G major scale. This key contains the note F#, which is played on fret 2 of the second (E) string.

- Bars 6, 7 and 8 feature dotted eighth notes. These give a distinctive skip to the rhythm in these bars, that distinguish them from the straight rhythm used in other bars. Listen to the CD to hear how these sound.

LISTEN AND LEARN: Galway Gallop can be heard on CD track 8

Free Choice Specialism

There are four options to choose from in this section of the exam, and you are free to select whichever <u>ONE</u> option you prefer.

Option 1 – Free Choice Piece:
You select a piece of your own choice.

The piece can be either in the format of a melody, or a solo piece, or a strummed or fingerstyle accompaniment to a song (backing tracks cannot be used). If you wish to sing whilst playing that is perfectly acceptable, but only the ukulele playing (not the singing) will be assessed.

When selecting a free choice piece, you should ensure that the chosen piece is of at least a similar technical standard and duration to the melodies or rhythm studies presented in this handbook. RGT will not advise on the suitability of free choice pieces as part of the assessment process here includes a candidate's ability to research and select an appropriate piece to perform.

OR

Option 2 – Another Handbook Melody:
You can select and perform another melody from those provided in the Performance chapter of this handbook.

If choosing this option, the melody that is performed must be different from that played in the Performance section of the exam.

OR

Option 3 – Another Rhythm Study:
You can select another Rhythm Study from the Rhythm Study chapter of this handbook.

This chord chart should then be performed either using the notated strum pattern provided with it during the first verse or, if you prefer, you can use a musically appropriate rhythm of your own choosing, providing that it is of at least a similar technical standard to the notated rhythms. In either case, some rhythmic variation should be used during the repeat section, as outlined in the Rhythm Study chapter of this handbook.

If selecting this option, the chord chart that is performed must be different from that played in the Rhythm Study and the Performance sections of the exam.

Option 4 – Fingerstyle Study:

You can perform the Fingerstyle Study notated below.

This consists of a chord progression that should be played using a repeated *'amim'* fingerpicking pattern twice per bar for the first four bars.

(*a* = third finger; *m* = middle finger; *i* = index finger; *p* = thumb.)

The abbreviation 'sim', under bar 2, means "continue in a similar way" – in other words, keep playing the same fingerpicking pattern for each chord.

The piece should be played with an even eighth note rhythm per bar.

From bar five onwards, the same picking pattern is used but, at the start and middle of each bar, the fourth string is also picked using the thumb (at the same time as the third finger picks the first string).

Notice that there are two chords in bar 11, and that after bar 11 the piece should be repeated from the beginning.

In the final bar the strings can either be plucked together or strummed once.

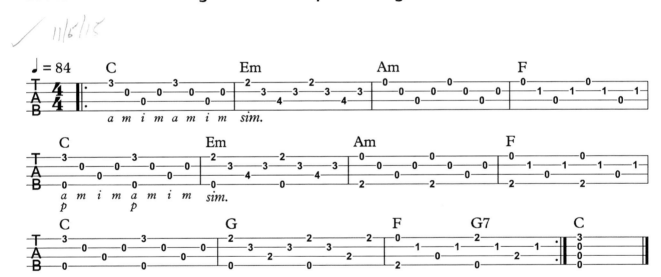

LISTEN AND LEARN: Option 4, Fingerstyle Study, can be heard on CD track 9

20

Prepared Accompaniment

You should select <u>ONE</u> of the three tunes provided in this chapter and play an accompaniment along with it using the chord chart provided. Each tune is performed on the CD that accompanies this handbook – this enables you not only to hear how each tune sounds, but also allows you to practise your accompaniment as much as you wish with the tune in advance of the exam.

In the exam, the examiner will play your selected tune (either via a recording or live on guitar or keyboard) and you should play a suitable chordal accompaniment to this selected tune.

You do not need to play from memory; you may use your handbook during this section of the exam. Remember to bring your handbook to the exam if you do not intend to play from memory; photocopies will not be permitted.

You can choose to either strum or/and fingerpick. The style of accompaniment, including the rhythms that you use, is left to your discretion and the examiner will not advise on this. The standard of playing is expected to be broadly equivalent to the strumming patterns in the Rhythm Study chapter or the fingerpicking in the Fingerstyle Study in the previous chapter. If you play something much simpler this will be reflected in the mark awarded.

Each tune is in either $^4_4$ or $^3_4$ time and is 8 bars in length (plus a final closing bar). As on the recording, there will be a verbal one-bar count-in before the tune is played through once. This initial 'practice' playing is just to remind you of the tune and its timing. Another verbal one-bar count-in will then be given straightaway and the main 8-bar tune will then be played twice *without stopping*, before ending on the final closing bar note. You will only be assessed during your playing in the final two verses – so you can use the first verse either just to listen or to practise (for example, by just strumming a chord once on the first beat of each bar so that you can get a feel for the timing).

The range of chords that may occur in this section of the exam is the same as those previously listed in the Rhythm Study chapter – i.e. A, Bb, C, D, F, G, Am, Dm, Em, F#m, Gm, Gm7, Cmaj7, A7, C7, D7, E7 and G7. You can view the fretboxes for the chords in the Rhythm Study chapter. In each chord chart each chord will last for one bar, with the exception of one 'split-bar' in which there will be two different chords (a diagonal line after a chord symbol in a split-bar indicates an additional beat for that chord). The chord in the very final bar (after the repeat) should be played with a single strum.

The tunes and chord charts are shown on the following pages. The notation for the tunes is provided in this handbook primarily for situations where a teacher might wish to play the tune with a student rather than use the CD provided.

ACCOMPANIMENT NO. 1

Accompaniment Chord Chart No.1

| 4/4 :‖ F | Dm | B♭ | C |

| F | Gm7 | Am | C / C7 / :‖ F |

Accompaniment Tune No. 1 **CD Track 10**

♩ = 112

ACCOMPANIMENT NO. 2

Accompaniment Chord Chart No. 2

| 4/4 :‖ C | E7 | A / A7 / | A |

| D | D7 | G | G7 :‖ C |

Accompaniment Tune No. 2 **CD Track 11**

♩ = 116

ACCOMPANIMENT NO. 3
Accompaniment Chord Chart No. 3

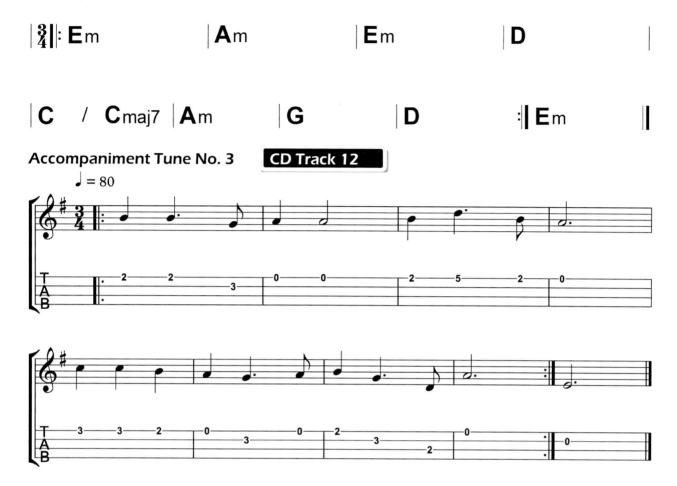

| $\frac{3}{4}$: Em | | Am | | Em | | D | |

| C / Cmaj7 | Am | | G | | D | : Em | |

Accompaniment Tune No. 3   CD Track 12

♩ = 80

Accompaniment Advice

1. Wait until you are totally comfortable playing all the chord shapes and changing between them fluently before attempting to practise your accompaniment to the tune on the CD.

2. Remember that the first time the tune is played you have the opportunity to either listen to it without needing to play along or to practise your timing by just strumming once on the first beat of each bar.

3. In the remaining two verses use an appropriate rhythm that suits the timing and style of the tune. Try to identify any prominent rhythmic elements of the melody and reflect these in your accompaniment. For instance if a particular bar or bars feature an obvious and distinctive rhythm, you might try to emulate this rhythm in your accompaniment.

4. Try to include some variation in your accompaniment, and particularly try to include some variation to differentiate your playing in the final verse from the previous verse.

5. Keep listening closely to the tune while playing your accompaniment and make sure to keep in time with it. Try to ensure that your chord changes come in clearly on the first beat of each bar, to help establish a definite pulse and rhythm.

6. Pay attention to how the chords sound and check that all the strings are ringing out clearly, without fretbuzz or unintended muted notes.

7. If you make a mistake, avoid the temptation to stop as you could lose your place in the music and fall out of time with the tune – particularly as the tune will carry on without you. If you cannot change to a chord in time, try placing your fretting hand across the strings to mute them whilst you carry on strumming until you can find your place in the music again – it's not ideal, but it will sound preferable to a total halt and the risk of losing your co-ordination with the tune.

Musicianship

The examiner will conduct a short selection of tests to assess your aural awareness, musical knowledge and knowledge of the instrument. The tests may be played by the examiner either live on guitar or keyboard or on ukulele via a recording. Descriptions and examples of the tests are provided below.

AURAL AWARENESS

Rhythm & Chord Tests

The examiner will play a two-bar chord progression in $^4_4$ time with a one-bar rhythm pattern; the rhythm pattern will be the same in each bar. The progression will consist of either a major chord followed by a minor chord, or a minor chord followed by a major chord. After hearing the progression played the first time you should clap the one-bar rhythm pattern that was used. (You should only clap the one-bar rhythm once.) The examiner will then play the same chord progression again and, without using your instrument, you will be asked to state whether the chords were major followed by minor, or minor followed by major.

In the exam, one rhythm and chord test will be given. The test may be played by the examiner either live on guitar or keyboard or on a ukulele via a recording. You should try to give your answers promptly and confidently.

Below are some *examples* of the type of tests that will be given.

Example 1:

Example 2:

MUSICAL KNOWLEDGE

The examiner will select one of the melodies or one of the rhythm studies that you have played previously in the exam and ask you to name both the key signature and time signature.

The time signature is given at the start of each melody and rhythm study and, for this grade, will either be $^3_4$ time or $^4_4$ time.

To identify the key signature of a rhythm study look at the chord in the first and very last bar. For each rhythm study the first and final chord will be the same, and this chord is the key chord of the study. For instance, Rhythm Study No.1 starts and finishes with an E minor chord and so the key is E minor.

The accompanying text for each of the melodies identifies the key in each case.

KNOWLEDGE OF THE INSTRUMENT

Notes On The Fretboard
The examiner will ask you to name a note from the range of notes shown in the diagram below. For instance, the examiner might ask: "What note is on the 2nd fret of the A string". The answer would be B.

This diagram is for practise only and should not be referred to during the exam itself.

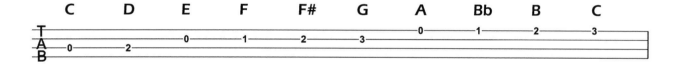

The range of notes reflects the notes that have occurred within the melodies of this and previous grades up to the third fret.

'Enharmonic equivalent' answers, such as A# instead of the Bb in the list above, will be fully acceptable in this instance.

Although the assessment here will focus primarily on accuracy, you also need to demonstrate a confident knowledge of the note names; therefore, the examiner will also consider the promptness of your response when assessing and marking this section of the exam.

Parts Of The Ukulele

The examiner will ask you to identify the location of one of the parts of the ukulele shown on the illustration below. You will not be allowed to refer to this handbook during this section of the exam, so you need to memorise the location of these parts of the ukulele.

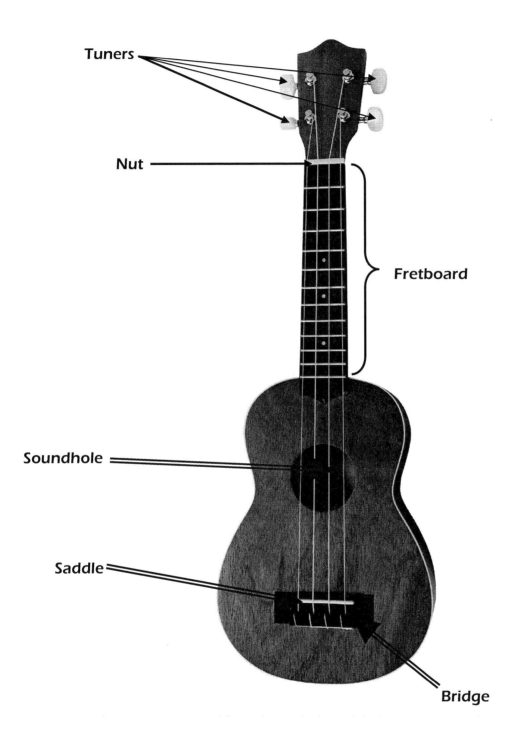

Appropriate and commonly used alternative names will be accepted. For example, 'fingerboard' instead of 'fretboard', and 'tuning heads' or 'tuning pegs' or 'tuning keys' or 'machine heads' instead of 'tuners'. However, the (normally dark wood) 'bridge' should not be confused with the (normally white plastic/bone) 'saddle'.

RGT®
Registry of Guitar Tutors
Exam Entry Form
Ukulele Grade ②

ONLINE ENTRY – AVAILABLE FOR UK CANDIDATES ONLY

For **UK candidates**, entries and payments can be made online at www.RGT.org, using the entry code below. You will be able to pay the entry fee by credit or debit card at a secure payment page on the website. Your unique and confidential exam entry code is:

UB-6621-AR

Keep this unique code confidential, as it can only be used once. Once you have entered online, you should sign this form overleaf. **You must bring this signed form to your exam and hand it to the examiner in order to be admitted to the exam room.**

If NOT entering online, please complete BOTH sides of this form and return to the address overleaf.

SESSION (Spring/Summer/Winter): _____ YEAR: _____

Dates/times NOT available: _____

Note: Only name *specific* dates (and times on those dates) when it would be <u>absolutely impossible</u> for you to attend due to important prior commitments (such as pre-booked overseas travel) which cannot be cancelled. We will then endeavour to avoid scheduling an exam session in your area on those dates. In fairness to all other candidates in your area, **only list dates on which it would be impossible for you to attend.** An entry form that blocks out unreasonable periods may be returned. (Exams may be held on any day of the week including, but not exclusively, weekends. Exams may be held within or outside of the school term.)

Candidate Details: *Please write as clearly as possible using BLOCK CAPITALS*

Candidate Name (as to appear on certificate): _____

Address: _____

_____ Postcode: _____

Tel. No. (day): _____ (mobile): _____

IMPORTANT: Take care to write your email address below as clearly as possible, as your exam entry acknowledgement and your exam appointment details will be sent to this email address. Only provide an email address that is in regular monitored use.

Email:_____

Where an email address is provided your exam correspondence will be sent by email only, and not by post. This will ensure your exam correspondence will reach you sooner.

Teacher Details *(if applicable)*

Teacher Name (as to appear on certificate): _____

RGT Tutor Code (if applicable):_____

Address: _____

_____ Postcode: _____

Tel. No. (day): _____ (mobile): _____

Email:_____

RGT Ukulele Official Entry Form

The standard LCM entry form is NOT valid for RGT exam entries.
Entry to the exam is only possible via this original form.
Photocopies of this form will not be accepted under any circumstances.

- Completion of this entry form is an agreement to comply with the current syllabus requirements and conditions of entry published at www.RGT.org. Where candidates are entered for exams by a teacher, parent or guardian that person hereby takes responsibility that the candidate is entered in accordance with the current syllabus requirements and conditions of entry.

- If you are being taught by an *RGT registered* tutor, please hand this completed form to your tutor and request him/her to administer the entry on your behalf.

- For candidates with special needs, a letter giving details should be attached.

Exam Fee: £_____ Late Entry Fee (if applicable): £_____

Total amount submitted: £_____

Cheques or postal orders should be made payable to Registry of Guitar Tutors.

Details of conditions of entry, entry deadlines and exam fees are obtainable from the RGT website: www.RGT.org

Once an entry has been accepted, entry fees cannot be refunded.

CANDIDATE INFORMATION (UK Candidates only)

In order to meet our obligations in monitoring the implementation of equal opportunities policies, UK candidates are required to supply the information requested below. The information provided will in no way whatsoever influence the marks awarded during the exam.

Date of birth: _____ Age: _____ Gender – please circle: male / female

Ethnicity (please enter 2 digit code from chart below): _____ Signed: _____

ETHNIC ORIGIN CLASSIFICATIONS (If you prefer not to say, write '17' in the space above.)

White: **01 British**   **02 Irish**   **03 Other white background**

Mixed: **04 White & black Caribbean**   **05 White & black African**   **06 White & Asian**   **07 Other mixed background**

Asian or Asian British: **08 Indian**   **09 Pakistani**   **10 Bangladeshi**   **11 Other Asian background**

Black or Black British: **12 Caribbean**   **13 African**   **14 Other black background**

Chinese or Other Ethnic Group: **15 Chinese**   **16 Other**   **17 Prefer not to say**

I understand and accept the current syllabus regulations and conditions of entry for this exam as specified on the RGT website.

Signed by candidate (if aged 18 or over) _____ Date _____

If candidate is under 18, this form should be signed by a parent/guardian/teacher (circle which applies):

Signed _____ Name_____ Date_____

UK ENTRIES

See overleaf for details of how to enter online OR return this form to:
Registry of Guitar Tutors, Registry Mews, 11 to 13 Wilton Road, Bexhill-on-Sea, E. Sussex, TN40 1HY
(If you have submitted your entry online do NOT post this form, instead you need to sign it above and hand it to the examiner on the day of your exam.)
To contact the RGT office telephone 01424 222222 or Email office@RGT.org

NON-UK ENTRIES

To locate the address within your country that entry forms should be sent to, and to view exam fees in your currency, visit the RGT website **www.RGT.org** and navigate to the 'RGT Worldwide' section.